<u>*In Dedication:*</u> Written and dedicated to the countless people who serve Sunday after Sunday, furthering the Gospel message. May you be richly blessed by the Lord, in many ways, as you serve Him using your gifts and talents.

"Therefore, my dear brothers and sisters, stand firm. Let nothing move you. Always give yourselves fully to the work of the Lord, because you know that your labor in the Lord is not in vain."
<u>**1 Corinthians 15:58, NIV**</u>

Philippians-Joy in Action Study Guide

Library of Congress Control Number: 2025913086

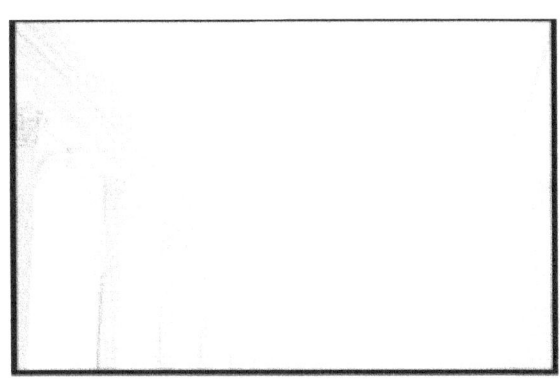

Philippians –
Joy in Action

FRANK & SAMUEL GERVASI

MIDWEST CHRISTIAN PUBLISHING

Study Guide-Part 1

ISBN: 979-8-9985125-9-9

Philippians-Joy in Action Study Guide

Introduction:

The church at Philippi was started, during the Apostle Paul's third missionary journey, around 50 or 51 AD. They were definitely not a perfect church but one that was close to his heart.

The Apostle Paul had started it with some of his friends, so he cared deeply about them. The letter itself is known as one of the Prison Epistles. Yet, even under these circumstances he remained joyful and content. Giving us today thousands of years later a blueprint for the right living.

Our hope and prayer are that you faithfully dig in for the next 30-Lessons as we examine, apply, and grow in faith and joy in the:

Philippians-Joy in Action Study Guide.

Table of Contents

Lesson #1 - The Fruit of Thankfulness
Read: *Philippians 1:3-11*

Memory Verse: *"...so that you may be able to discern what is best and may be pure and blameless for the day of Christ, filled with the fruit of righteousness that comes through Jesus Christ — to the glory and praise of God."*
Philippians 1:10-11, NIV

Open in Prayer

The popularity and availability of fresh fruit in everyday life has increased dramatically in the last 50 years. This expanded inventory (9,000 items in the 1970s to almost 50,000 items today) means a far more diverse and vibrant range of fruits and vegetables to choose from. However, some take center stage, particularly the banana, America's #1 most-purchased fruit. America's best-loved fruit earned its top spot thanks to the convenience it offers, as well as its versatility. Easy to store in a lunch box or at the bottom of a backpack, the banana is a great snack to enjoy on the go. Bananas are also well known for their high levels of the mood-enhancing chemical tryptophan, making them literally a good fruit. Coming in after bananas at the top, apples, strawberries, and grapes came in 2nd, 3rd, and 4th most purchased (respectively). 1

1. How would you define thankfulness? (Explain) _____
_____
_____
_____

Read Philippians 1:3-11: 3

"I thank my God every time I remember you. 4 In all my prayers for all of you, I always pray with joy 5 because of your partnership in the gospel from the first day until now, 6 being confident of this, that he who began a good work in you will carry it on to completion until the day of Christ Jesus. 7 It is right for me to feel this way about all of you, since I have you in my heart and, whether I am in chains or defending and confirming the gospel, all of you share in God's grace with me. 8 God can testify how I long for all of you with the affection of Christ Jesus. 9 And this is my prayer: that your love may abound more and more in knowledge and depth of insight, 10 so that you may be able to discern what is best and may be pure and blameless for the day of Christ, 11 filled with the fruit of righteousness that comes through Jesus Christ—to the glory and praise of God."

Big Idea: A thankful spirit produces spiritual fruit in us that glorifies God.

----

2. What words does the Apostle Paul use to reveal his attitude towards the church at Philippi? *(Explain)* _____

_____

_____

This church in Philippi – which the Apostle Paul is addressing in these verses – knew Paul well, and vice versa. That's why Paul was so thankful for them and wanted the best for them. Verses 10 & 11 tells us specifically what he desires for this group of believers: *"...so that you may be able to discern what is best and may be pure and blameless for the day of Christ, filled with the fruit of righteousness that comes through Jesus Christ—to the glory and praise of God."* (NIV)

3. What do the following verses show about being thankful?

1 Corinthians 10:30:	
Colossians 2:7:	
Colossians 3:15:	
Colossians 4:2:	

The church at Philippi had already been living out their faith in a way that was noticeable in producing fruit. Paul considered them his *"partners...in the Gospel"* (v. 5) and that they *"shared in God's grace with [him]"* (v. 7).

But Paul also desired them to grow, rooted in this same sense of contagious and invincible joy that he himself had. He specifically desired that: *"...your love may abound more and more in knowledge and depth of insight..."* (v. 9)

_____

Insight: When the church is rooted in Christ and living with thankful and joyful mindsets, God will always get the glory.

_____

4. What are reasons I have to be Thankful today? (Be specific)

A. _____ B. _____
C. _____ D. _____

Now, some may say that the *"fruit of righteousness"* in our passage is talking about our being made right positionally through salvation, because of the phrase *"through Christ"*. However, it is more likely that he is speaking about the fruit of spiritual growth produced from being grounded in Christ.

5. What stands out in the following verses about righteousness? (Explain your reasons)

Psalm 5:8:	
Psalm 7:8:	
Matthew 5:6-10:	
Matthew 6:1:	
John 16:8-10:	
Romans 3:21-26:	

Finally, notice the end of verse 11: *"...to the glory and praise God."* The Philippians' life of joyful surrender and obedience to God gave Him the honor He deserved. Let's do the same, choosing to cultivate a mindset of joy, leading to spiritual growth, for the glory and praise of God.

6. What are ways we can bring glory to God in my everyday life? (Be specific) _____
A. _____
B. _____
C. _____

1. *Where am I finding my joy?*_____
_____
_____

2. *In what ways am I growing in my walk with Jesus?*_____
_____
_____

3. *What ways need improvement in my walk?*_____
_____
_____

Going Deeper Section:

What is the significance of the *"fruits of righteousness"* in our passage? In **Matthew Henry's Commentary on the Whole Bible**, Henry sheds some light on what these fruits are and how we can acquire them.

"These verses contain the prayers [Paul] put up for them. Paul often let his friends know what it was he begged of God for them, that they might know what to beg for themselves and be directed in their own prayers...He prayed...[t]hat they might be a fruitful useful people... The fruits of righteousness are the evidence and effects of our sanctification, the duties of holiness springing from a renewed heart...Observe [that] Those who do much good should still endeavor to do more. The fruits of righteousness, brought forth for the glory of God and edification of his church, should really fill us, and wholly take us up. Fear not being emptied by bringing forth the fruits of righteousness, for you will be filled with them. These fruits are by Jesus Christ, by his strength and grace, for without him we can do nothing."[2]

_____

Going Deeper Response:

First, identify 3 Things you should be thankful for. Then, list 3 areas that you need to be more grateful. Then lift each one up in prayer or Thank God for the ones you are grateful for.

Pray: Asking God to help us take joy in Him and make my life am offering of worship...

_____

Lesson written by Pastor Frank & Samuel Gervasi

_____

1. Adapted from *What is the Most Commonly Consumed Fruit in the US?*, as accessed at https://www.buffalomarket.com/blogs/news/most-commonly-consumed-fruit-in-the-us#:~:text=Bananas.%20America's%20best%2Dloved%20fruit%20earned%20its%20top,concentration %20of%20natural%20fructose%20and%20quick%2Drelease%20energy., on 12/26/2024.

2. *Matthew Henry's Commentary on the Whole Bible*, public domain, as accessed on Bible Gateway Plus, on 12/26/2024.

Philippians-Joy in Action Study Guide

Lesson: #2 - A Plan Behind the Cloud
Read: *Philippians 1:12-14*

__Memory Verse:__ "...[i]n the same way, the gospel is bearing fruit and growing throughout the whole world—just as it has been doing among you since the day you heard it and truly understood God's grace."
Colossians 1:6b, NIV

Open in Prayer

Newscaster Paul Harvey tells a story of God's providential care over thousands of allied prisoners during World War II. One of America's B-29 bombers took off from the island of Guam with its eyes set on a target in Kokura, Japan. However, because clouds covered the target area, the aircraft circled for nearly an hour until its fuel supply reached the danger point. The captain and his crew finally decided they had better go after the secondary target. Changing course, they found that the sky was clear, dropped their payload, and headed for home base. Sometime later an officer received some startling information from military intelligence. Just one week before the pilots' mission, the Japanese had transferred one of their largest concentrations of captured Americans to the city of Kokura – the original target of the bomber! Upon reading this, the officer exclaimed, *"Thank God for that protecting cloud! If the city hadn't been hidden from the bomber, it would have been destroyed."*[1]

That thick cloud over Kokura, Japan, was certainly a surprising and unwelcome obstacle to the pilots, but because of it, many lives were saved. We too encounter obstacles and difficulties in life, but as we'll see in our devotion today, God can use those difficulties to give us an opportunity to change lives.

Philippians-Joy in Action Study Guide

<u>Read Philippians 1:12-14:</u>

"Now I want you to know, brothers and sisters,[a] that what has happened to me has actually served to advance the gospel. 13 As a result, it has become clear throughout the whole palace guard[b] and to everyone else that I am in chains for Christ. 14 And because of my chains, most of the brothers and sisters have become confident in the Lord and dare all the more to proclaim the gospel without fear." (NIV)

_____

<u>Big Idea</u>: Our hardships can give us an opportunity to advance the Gospel.

_____

1. How would you define hardship? (Be specific) _____
_____
_____
_____

At the time of writing this letter, the Apostle Paul wasn't exactly able to go out into the streets or into people's homes to tell them about Jesus. Paul wrote the book of Philippians from prison.

However, instead of hindering the advancement of the Good News, this development was only working to help, as Paul tells us in v. 12: *"Now I want you to know, brothers and sisters, that what has happened to me has actually served to advance the gospel."* (NIV)

2. What times or situations do you find it hard to share the Gospel? *(Explain your answers)* _____
_____
_____
_____

3. What do the following verses show about sharing the Gospel?

Matthew 4:23:	
Matthew 9:35:	
Matthew 24:14:	
Acts 15:7:	
Acts 20:24:	

4. How helpful exactly was Paul's imprisonment? *(Be specific)*

1. _____
2. _____
3. _____
4. _____

Well, for one, verse 13 brings up the *"whole palace guard"* – which probably consisted of a few thousand soldiers. Paul had the opportunity to speak to the guards who watched him about Christ, and he may have already had some experience with them from when he was persecuting the church. Word got around, and soon all the troops knew about Paul's faith in Jesus.

————————

Insight: *Because hardships can lead to sharing the Gospel, we should not be surprised but rather be practical and willing.*

————————

In addition, Acts 28:30 (which describes Paul's imprisonment) says that Paul *"...welcomed everyone who came to see him."* During the time of his imprisonment, Paul was under house arrest. This meant that Paul could not go out, but others could come to him. And Paul used these opportunities to spread the Gospel.

5. What difficulties or challenges have resulted because of your faith? *(Be specific)* ___

_____
_____
_____

6 What do the following verses show about hardship and difficulties?

Acts 14:22:	
2 Corinthians 6:3-4:	
2 Corinthains 12:10:	
Revelation 2:3:	

Whatever difficulty we face today, whether it be stress at work, a sickness or ailment, an issue with a bill, or anything else, God could be giving you an opportunity to advance the Good News!

————————

Philippians-Joy in Action Study Guide

1. What opportunities do I have to advance the Gospel today? _____
_____
_____
_____

2. What ways can I advance the Gospel in m y everyday life? _____
_____
_____
_____

3. What anxieties do I have about sharing the Gospel message and my faith?
_____
_____
_____
_____

Going Deeper Section:

What does it mean that Paul's imprisonment made his fellow believers *"confident in the Lord"* (v. 14)? The **NIV Quest Study Bible Notes** offers its interpretation, and in so doing, gives us an encouragement to be bold as well:

"Courage can be contagious. The world of the early church was not always friendly to the gospel. But even during great hardship, Paul ignored the potential negative consequences and shared the message anyway. His example challenged other believers to be just as bold in proclaiming the gospel." [2]

Lesson written by Pastor Frank & Samuel Gervasi

---

1. Adapted from a story told by John Nelson Darby, as accessed on https://www.sermonillus trations.com/a-z/g/god_sovereignty.htm, on 1/02/2024.
2. *NIV Quest Study Bible Notes*, Copyright © 1994, 2003, 2011 by Zondervan, as accessed on Bible Gateway Plus, on 1/02/2024.

Philippians-Joy in Action Study Guide

Lesson #3 - Motives Matter
Read: *Philippians 1:15-18*

_____

Memory Verse: *"But what does it matter? The important thing is that in every way, whether from false motives or true, Christ is preached. And because of this, I rejoice. Yes, and I will continue to rejoice..."* **Philippians 1:18, NIV**

Open in Prayer:

"At the village church in Kalonovka, Russia, attendance at Sunday school picked up after the priest started handing out candy to the peasant children. One of the most faithful was a pug-nosed kid who recited his Scriptures with proper piety, pocketed his reward, then fled into the fields to munch on it. But the priest took a liking to the boy and persuaded him to attend church school. By offering other inducements, the priest managed to teach the boy the four Gospels. In fact, he won a special prize for learning all four by heart and reciting them nonstop in church. 60 years down the road, the young boy still likes to recite Scriptures, but in a context that would horrify his old priest. The prize pupil, who memorized so much of the Bible, was Nikita Khrushchev, the former Communist czar. The same Nikita Khrushchev who nimbly mouthed God's Word when a child, later declared God to be nonexistent because his cosmonauts had not seen Him. It seems that the "why" behind memorization is equally important as the "what"; artificial motivation will produce artificial results." 1

The intentions behind why we do the right thing matters to God. And as we'll see in our devotion today, we should have the proper motives when we tell others about Jesus.

Read the passage: *__Philippians 1:15-18__*

"It is true that some preach Christ out of envy and rivalry, but others out of goodwill. 16 The latter do so out of love, knowing that I am put here for the defense of the gospel. 17 The former preach Christ out of selfish ambition, not sincerely, supposing that they can stir up trouble for me while I am in chains. 18 But what does it matter? The important thing is that in every way, whether from false motives or true, Christ is preached. And because of this I rejoice. Yes, and I will continue to rejoice." (NIV)

_____

Big Idea: Our motives for sharing the Gospel are important, so we should analyze what our intentions are.

_____

1. What are common reasons people might have to do something for someone else?

A. _____   B. _____

C. _____   D. _____

E. _____

In our passage, the Apostle Paul lists two contrasting motivations behind why believers in the Philippian church were preaching the Gospel.

Some *"...preach[ed] Christ out of envy and rivalry..." (v. 15, NIV.)* They told others about the Good News because Paul was receiving recognition for his efforts, and they wanted to be better than him – to be competitive.

2. What do the following passages show about reasons for doing something?

Philippians 3:3-5:	
1 Timothy 1:13-15:	
1 John 2:12-13:	

However, in addition to these selfish evangelists, were a group of people who told others about Jesus "out of goodwill" (v. 15, NIV). The phrase "out of goodwill" carries with it the idea of being rooted in love.

Philippians-Joy in Action Study Guide

3. What would be some proper motivations to share the Gospel? (Be specific)

A. _____ B. _____

C. _____ D. _____

These believers shared their faith as an overflow of love toward God for what they had been given in Christ.

_____

Insight: Our motivation in sharing the Gospel should be not to further our own name or reputation, but the glory of Jesus' name, out of gratitude for all that He's done in our lives.

_____

4. What do the following passages say was the cause of gratitude for each situation?

Psalm 100:1-3:	
Psalm 147:6-8:	
Jonah 2:9:	
Romans 16:3:	

5. What are reasons someone might not Talk about God's kingdom more? (Be detailed as possible) _____

_____

_____

_____

The Apostle Paul looked at the situation with the Philippian church from another angle. Even though some preached the Gospel with impure motives, the name of Jesus was still going forward rapidly and powerfully, and Paul rejoiced in it!

Verse 18 says, "But what does it matter? The important thing is that in every way, whether from false motives or true, Christ is preached. And because of this, I rejoice. Yes, and I will continue to rejoice..."

Philippians-Joy in Action Study Guide

Because God is sovereign and in control, He can use even our bad motives to accomplish His purposes. But if we have experienced the goodness and grace of God, how could we continue sharing our faith for the wrong reasons? Our motives matter to God; let's have the proper ones when we share our faith.

Challenge Section:

1. What intentions do I typically have when I share the Gospel? _____

_____

_____

_____

2. Am I doing it out of gratitude or other improper motives? Yes or No
(Explain) _____

_____

_____

_____

3. What things can help me share my faith more? _____

_____

_____

_____

Philippians-Joy in Action Study Guide

Going Deeper Section:

The NIV Grace and Truth Study Bible notes this about Philippians 1:15-18a: "Into Paul's encouraging report of Christians emboldened by his captivity to speak the gospel, the apostle inserts a surprising caveat: some preach Christ as Paul's competitors, imagining that their success will frustrate him, making his chains chafe, as it were. Paul describes their motives as envy, rivalry, and selfish ambition, anticipating the caution he will register against self-centered, competitive attitudes that could endanger the Philippians' solidarity with one another (2:1–4). Paul fiercely opposed rival Christian teachers when they distorted the gospel of God's grace into a different message that did not deserve to be called good news (Gal 1:6–9; 5:7–12; 6:12–13) or if their character contradicted Christ's purity (Php 3:18–19; 2Co 11:1–15). Paul readily rejoices in the evangelistic success of his rivals at Rome, so we conclude that, despite their unworthy motives, their message was true to Christ and his grace. Therefore, contrary to their expectation, Paul finds reason to rejoice when their proclamation of Christ yields fruit in changed lives. Thus, Paul sets the pace for Philippians in selfless commitment to Christ's glory, not to one's own reputation. As he does elsewhere, Paul characterizes the gospel as preaching Christ, for the divine Son who became human and his redemptive achievement are the message that brings salvation (Ro 1:2–4; 1Co 1:23–24,30; 2:2–4; Col 1:28)." 2

Going Deeper Response:

List three friends, acquaintances, or family members that you can share the Gospel with. Once identified plan a specific time you can meet with them for coffee and share your faith.

Pray: *Asking God to help me spread the Gospel with pure intentions and the power of His Holy Spirit...*

———————————

Lesson written by Pastor Frank & Samuel Gervasi

———————————

1. *Adapted from a story told by Parade Magazine 1962, as accessed on https://www.sermonillustrations.com/a-z/m/motivation.htm, on 1/05/2024.*
2. *NIV Grace and Truth Study Bible, Copyright © 2021 by Zondervan, all rights reserved, as accessed on Bible Gateway Plus, on 1/05/2024.*

Philippians-Joy in Action Study Guide

Lesson #4 - Eternal Priorities
Read: *Philippians 1:19-24*

_____

Memory Verse: *"For to me, to live is Christ and to die is gain."*
Philippians 1:21, NIV

Open in Prayer:

"*In* past *years there was a* football *coach who divorced his wife of 26 years when he left* the college ranks *to become head coach in the National Football League. He said he* needed *a wife while coaching on the college level for social functions, and to show families that he would be looking out for their sons. In pro football,* however, *she was an unnecessary* responsibility *and a distraction to winning. He said winning football was his number one priority and his two sons second;* she simply had to be cut out. *In contrast to this, Tom Landry, former coach of the Dallas Cowboys said, "The thrill of knowing Jesus is the greatest thing that ever happened to me...I think God has put me in a very special place, and He expects me to use it to His glory in everything I do...whether coaching football or talking to the press, I'm always a Christian...Christ is first, family second and football third."*[1]

(Adapted from a story told by an unknown author, as accessed on https://www.sermonillustrations.com/a-z/p/priorities.htm, on 1/09/2024)
These two coaches obviously had very different philosophies when it came to what they prioritized. Likewise, we all must make a choice what is most important to us. And as we'll see in our devotion today, our Heavenly Father deserves to be the first priority in the lives of each of His children.

Read *Philippians 1:19-24*

"For I know that through your prayers and God's provision of the Spirit of Jesus Christ what has happened to me will turn out for my deliverance.[a] 20 I eagerly expect and hope that I will in no way be ashamed, but will have sufficient courage so that now as always Christ will be exalted in my body, whether by life or by death. 21 For to me, to live is Christ and to die is gain. 22 If I am to go on living in the body, this will mean fruitful labor for me. Yet what shall I choose? I do not know! 23 I am torn between the two: I desire to depart and be with Christ, which is better by far; 24 but it is more necessary for you that I remain in the body." (NIV)

———————————

Big Idea: *Living out our faith and furthering the Gospel should be our highest priority.*

———————————

1. What does it mean to live for something? _____

_____

_____

_____

In our passage, the Apostle Paul recognized that his imprisonment could lead either to his death, or to his release. And yet, Paul had confidence that whichever outcome would come to fruition, Christ would be glorified.

2. Do you think a person can bring glory to God? *(Explain your answers)* _____

_____

_____

_____

3. What do the following verses say about glorifying God?

Psalm 34:3:	
Psalm 63:3:	
Daniel 4:37:	
Matthew 5:16:	
Luke 2:20:	
Romans 15:6:	

4. What are ways that we can bring glory to God? *(Be specific)*

A. _____ B. _____
C. _____ D. _____

Verses 21 and 22a say, *"For to me, to live is Christ and to die is gain. If I am to go on living in the body, this will mean fruitful labor for me."* (NIV)

Paul knew well that when he died he would immediately experience the culmination of all he had hoped for – being in the physical presence of his Savior. However, if it were God's will for him to remain on earth, it would be for Paul to advance the Gospel. Which implies that if we are believers living on earth, our goal should be to advance the Gospel message in the same way.

5. What are ways we can advance the Gospel message in our life and culture around us?

A. _____ B. _____
C. _____ D. _____

_____

Insight: All believers should prioritize sharing the faith and doing God's will as the most important thing in their lives.

_____

Advancing the Gospel doesn't always look like leading someone to salvation or inviting them to church. Sometimes advancing the Gospel takes the form of meeting people's physical needs, or treating others with gentleness and compassion, while still always being *"...prepared to give an answer to everyone who asks you to give the reason for the hope that you have."* (1 Peter 3:15a, NIV)

6. What do the following verses say about accomplishing goals?

Romans 9:31:	
2 Corinthians 5:9:	
Philippians 3:12-14:	
Colossians 2:2:	
1 Timothy 1:5:	

"A Christian...should so shine in their life, that a person could not go a week without knowing the Gospel." Spurgeon

Philippians-Joy in Action Study Guide

May we make advancing the Gospel message of Christ a priority in our lives – today and always!

Challenge Section:

1. What things do I tend to give to greater priority than I should? *(Explain your answers)* _____
_____
_____
_____

2. How important is advancing the Gospel in my priorities? *Score yourself between 1-10) (1-Lowest and 10-Highest)* _____ *(Explain reason for that score)* _____
_____
_____
_____

3. What area of my life needs to be glorifying God better? *(Explain your reasoning)*
_____
_____
_____
_____

Going Deeper Section:

How could Paul be so joyful that he didn't even care whether he lived or died? In the **NIV Application Commentary**, Frank Thielman breaks it down for us, and in so doing, gives us an encouragement to lean on God's power and presence to help us see things through such a mind-boggling perspective:

"Paul explains more fully the reason for this remarkable indifference to his physical fate in the second part of the passage...Paul's account of his circumstances prior to verse 21 and his perspective on the future after this verse both demonstrate what his close relationship with Christ means in practical terms. Prior to verse 21, even imprisonment by the unbelieving authorities and ill will from fellow believers could not dampen the joyful character of Paul's life, for God was advancing the gospel of Jesus Christ through these hardships (1:12 - 18a). After verse 21, Paul looks ahead and comments that death is gain, for it will mean the closest possible union with Christ. In the same way, continued life is fruitful labor because it means that Paul will be able both to preach the gospel (1:7) and strengthen the Philippians' faith (1:25). Such a perspective on the hardships of the present and the possibility of the future **is possible for Paul only because Christ lives within him and gives him strength** *(4:13)."* [2]

Going Deeper Response:

Take a bible concordance and find several verses about the *future*. Then offer those areas to God in prayer.

Pray: Asking God to help me live out my faith for others to see Him through my actions...

_____

Lesson written by Pastor Frank & Samuel Gervasi

_____

1. Adapted from a story told by an unknown author, as accessed on https://www.sermonillustrations.com/a-z/p/priorities.htm, on 1/09/2024.
2. *NIV Application Commentary*, Copyright © 1995 by Frank Thielman., as accessed on Bible Gateway Plus, on 1/09/2024.

Lesson #5 - A Holy Boldness
Read: *Philippians 1:19-24*

Memory Verse: *"May I never boast except in the cross of our Lord Jesus Christ, through which the world has been crucified to me, and I to the world."*
Galatians 6:14, NIV

Open in Prayer:

Introduction:

Many Christians are afraid to tell others about the gospel for many reasons. Fears abound, images of the various responses of the people will tell, can surface. However, God tells us to share the Gospel message with others around on a regular basis. The ***Cambridge Dictionary*** defines boldness as this: *"willingness to take risks and act innovatively; confidence or courage."*[1]

However, if one thinks about it, God does not leave us to fend for ourselves when the task is before us. And as we will see in our devotion today, the Cross is where we can get our confidence, and bragging rights really belong to Him.

Philippians 1:19-24: *"For I know that through your prayers and God's provision of the Spirit of Jesus Christ what has happened to me will turn out for my deliverance.[a] 20 I eagerly expect and hope that I will in no way be ashamed, but will have sufficient courage so that now as always Christ will be exalted in my body, whether by life or by death. 21 For to me, to live is Christ and to die is gain. 22 If I am to go on living in the body, this will mean fruitful labor for me."*

"Yet what shall I choose? I do not know! 23 I am torn between the two: I desire to depart and be with Christ, which is better by far; 24 but it is more necessary for you that I remain in the body." **(NIV)**

Big Idea: **When Living Out the Gospel-All Boasting Should be in Christ**

---

1. What are things that people may commonly boast about? *(Be specific)*

A. _____ B. _____

C. _____ D. _____

The *Big Idea* means simply, that whether we are effective in bringing someone to Christ. Or we never see someone embrace the gospel and receive Christ. We are still called to be faithful.

2. What common things come to mind when you think about sharing your faith?
(Explain your answers) _____
_____
_____
_____

Looking at today's passage we see that very thing. And ultimately the result is in God's hand, anyway. Every time we share our faith and, every time we promote the Gospel of Christ. So, don't be discouraged, or feel that you're doing something wrong. The power of the Holy Spirit is what changes people's hearts. Because we read in v. 26: Pause
"Your boasting in Christ Jesus will abound."

3. What do the following bible texts say about God's Power in relation to the Gospel message?

Acts 3:12:	
Acts 4:7:	
Romans 1:16:	
Romans 4:21:	
1 Corinthians 1:18:	
1 Corinthians 2:5:	

Now, in this case it was because the Apostle Paul remained, and kind of looks a little prideful, because he says, *"on account of me."*

I read that and thought, wow! He's kind of full of himself!

However, I don't think he was boasting but more just acknowledging that the church was not that established and rooted for several years yet.

4. Do you believe that discipline and preparation are needed when sharing our faith and reaching others for the Gospel? (Explain your answer) _____

_____

_____

_____

In fact, even though the book of Philippians was written in AD 61 or so. The church at Philippi wasn't established until his second missionary journey. Making the church at Philippi, eight years old or so. Some church plants fall apart well after that time frame.

5. What do the following texts show additionally about God's power?

1 Corinthians 6:14:	
2 Corinthians 4:7:	
2 Corinthians 10:4:	
2 Corinthians 12:9:	
Ephesians 1:18-20:	

Consequently, people can impact a churches success or not. But ultimately, if God has ordained for that church or ministry to prosper and move forward it's better that it's in Christ that the boasting and bragging is done.

_____

Insight: When Living Out the Gospel-All Boasting Should Be in Christ-Because the Gospel's Power is in the Cross

_____

The apostle Paul understood that the crucifixion was where the power of the Gospel resided. Think about what he says in the epistle of Galatians. In chapter 6, where he was talking about putting confidence in the flesh, and doing those outward rituals to satisfy God in some way. In v. 14 he says, *"May I never boast except in the cross of our Lord Jesus Christ, through which the world has been crucified to me, and I to the world."* Meaning, he only wanted to be known for Christ crucified. Nothing else! Very straightforward!

Philippians-Joy in Action Study Guide

And nothing else matters or is more important than the gospel message. Either, people accept the message, or they don't. Our job is to be faithful, especially in how we live our lives for others to see.

_____

Greg Laurie says, "*He will not force you to share your faith, but He will prompt you. And when you take that step of faith, He will empower and use you.*"2

_____

Let's be faithful and share our faith today. Boasting in the Cross and leaving the results to God.

Challenge Section:

*1. Who have I shared my faith with recently?*_____

_____

_____

_____

2. Who can I talk with about the Cross of Christ this week?

A. _____ B. _____

C. _____ D. _____

E. _____ F. _____

3. Which neighbors can I seek to engage for the sake of the Gospel and sharing my faith?

A. _____ B. _____

C. _____ D. _____

E. _____ F. _____

Going Deeper Section:

The *Zondervan Bible Backgrounds Commentary* talks about the deliverance of Paul when it says, *"Will turn out for my deliverance ... and ... that I will in no way be ashamed (1:19–20). Although Paul nowhere indicates that he is quoting Scripture when he uses this phrase, it is a word-for-word citation of the Greek version of Job 13:16. Job says that he knows, contrary to his accusers, that his own iniquity is not the cause of his suffering. He uses the metaphor of standing trial before God and says that he is confident that after God has cross-examined him he will be saved. Similarly, Paul knows that whatever the outcome of his trial, when he stands before God he will have no cause for shame but will experience "salvation" (NIV, "deliverance")."* [3]

Going Deeper Response:

Think about it and identify what might embarrass us about sharing our faith. Then write a response to each item and how you might overcome it.

Pray: Asking God to help us boldly proclaim our faith for others to see Him through our lives...

———————————

Lesson written by Pastor Frank & Samuel Gervasi

———————————

1. Cambridge Dictionary, at https://dictionary.cambridge.org/us/dictionary/english/boldness accessed, on 01/12/2024.
2. *Greg Laurie, Tell Someone: You Can Share the Good News,* https://www.goodreads.com/work/quotes/45656479-tell-someone-you-can-share-the-good-news ,as accessed on 01/12/2024.
3. *Zondervan Bible Backgrounds Commentary,* Zondervan 2002, from www.biblegateway.com, as accessed on 01/12/2025.

Lesson #6 - Worthy Citizens
Read: *Philippians 1:27*

Memory Verse: *"Therefore, since we are surrounded by such a great cloud of witnesses, let us throw off everything that hinders and the sin that so easily entangles. And let us run with perseverance the race marked out for us..."*
Hebrews 12:1, NIV

Open in Prayer:

Introduction:

"*Howard Hendricks* once boarded *an American Airline flight after a very long delay.* One of Hendricks' fellow passengers, *who had too much to drink, was being rude to the other passengers*, and *demanding with the flight attendants*. One of the flight attendants on board tried to calm down the livid traveler and restore order in the plane. *Hendricks watched the flight attendant treat this unpleasant man with class, dignity and professionalism. She was unruffled. Howard was so impressed that he walked to the back of the plane* to praise her for her actions. *He told her how impressed he was* at her response, *and that he was going to write a letter of commendation to American Airlines. In response, she said, 'Thank you sir, but I don't work for American Airlines.' Hendricks was* momentarily confused *until she* clarified, *'I work for Jesus Christ.'*"[1]

This stewardess understood what it meant to let her faith shine through her actions and live with a higher perspective, and others noticed. We too have been called to live in a way that identifies us with Christ, and as we'll see in our devotion today, our understanding of being a citizen of God's kingdom is important if we are to live up to our calling.

Read Passage:

"Whatever happens, conduct yourselves in a manner worthy of the gospel of Christ. Then, whether I come and see you or only hear about you in my absence, I will know that you stand firm in the one Spirit,[a] striving together as one for the faith of the gospel." **(NIV)**

_____

Big Idea: As citizens of heaven, we should live in a way that shows others that we belong to Christ.

_____

In our passage today, the Apostle Paul exhorts the Philippians not just to talk about the Gospel, but to live it out. The first part of verse 27 says, *"Whatever happens, conduct yourselves in a manner worthy of the gospel of Christ."* (NIV)

1. What common ways do people conduct themselves in our culture today? (Be specific) _____

_____

_____

_____

2. What do the following verses show about a person's conduct?

Esther 1:17:	
Job 34:11:	
Psalm 112:5:	
Ecclesiastes 6:8:	
2 Corinthians 1:12:	
1 Timothy 3:15:	

More recent translations will often use the phrase *"...live as a citizen of heaven..."* (NLT), which sheds some light on this concept.

3. What ways are consistent with living as citizens of Heaven? (Explain) _____

_____

_____

_____

Any citizen has benefits that come with being a part of that country. For citizens of heaven, some of those benefits include being protected from harm, being given hope

Philippians-Joy in Action Study Guide

through the promises of Scripture, and the ability, in some circumstances, to make choices and choose the road we take.

Insight: All Christians are on display for unbelievers to watch, so we should conduct ourselves in a way that reflects well on who Jesus is and serves as an example to emulate.

---

4. What do the following texts say about watching others behavior?

Exodus 33:8:	
Deuteronomy 4:9-15:	
Joshua 4:11:	
Matthew 27:55:	
Mark 3:2:	

However, as much as citizenship in heaven is bursting with blessings, it also carries expectations. Just as any citizen must be prepared to defend the citizenship, so we must be prepared to defend the faith. Just as every citizen must remain loyal to their country, we must remain loyal to God and not take His blessings for granted. And just as every citizen is expected to handle their freedoms properly, we must use our freedom *"...[not] to indulge the flesh; rather, [to] serve one another humbly in love."* (Galatians 5:13, NIV)

5. What behaviors are in my life that need to be eradicated to be a better example to a watching World?

A. _____ B. _____
C. _____ D. _____
D. _____

"God created us for this: to live our lives in a way that makes him look more like the greatness and the beauty and the infinite worth that he really is."....John Piper

---

Let's be intentional to live out that purpose today, living in a way that shows we deserve to be identified as followers of Christ.

Challenge Section:

1. In what areas do I represent Christ in a positive light? _____
_____
_____
_____

2. In what areas is my conduct representing Him in a negative light? _____
_____
_____
_____
_____

3. What areas should I be conscious of my conduct in a greater way? _____
_____
_____
_____
_____

Going Deeper Section:

What does living "worthy of the Gospel" entail? The **NIV Biblical Theological Study Bible** expounds the following:

"Paul explains that this worthy living consists in standing united, refusing to be afraid of opponents, and being willing to suffer for the gospel." [2]

Going Deeper Response:

Define three areas where your witness is lacking. Then offer them up in prayer for God's strength to live them out......

Pray: Asking God to help me live a life worthy of being called a Christian...

Lesson written by Pastor Frank & Samuel Gervasi

---

1. Adapted from a story told by Ken Weliever, as accessed on https://thepreachersword.com/2019/09/02/word-of-the-week-work-2/, on 1/16/2025.
2. *NIV Biblical Theological Study Bible,* Copyright © 2019 by Zondervan, as accessed at Bible Gateway Plus, on 01/16/2025.

Lesson #7 - An Expected Opposition
Read: *Philippians 1:27b-28*

_____

Memory Verse: *"Don't be intimidated in any way by your enemies. This will be a sign to them that they are going to be destroyed, but that you are going to be saved, even by God himself."* **Philippians 1:28, NIV**

_____

Open in Prayer:

Introduction:

"Sometimes unexpected resistance can stop us.......Isn't that the way it always is when you start doing something you're excited about? Have you ever tackled a DIY project? Perhaps some craft......or home improvement project?......You thought, I can do that! You gathered the supplies, set time aside, and started on the project— but suddenly your work doesn't look like the picture....or.... (think the TV show Nailed It!), and you become discouraged. Or maybe it is harder than you expected, and you begin to think you've made a big mistake......" 1

We too experience opposition regarding our faith. People will sometime avoid us, want to argue, and even minimize our faith in Jesus Christ. As we continue in our study in the book of Philippians this month, the Apostle Paul reminds us of this very fact.

Read Philippians 1:27-28:

"Whatever happens, conduct yourselves in a manner worthy of the gospel of Christ. Then, whether I come and see you or only hear about you in my absence, I will know that you stand firm in the one Spirit, [a]"

"striving together as one for the faith of the gospel 28 without being frightened in any way by those who oppose you. This is a sign to them that they will be destroyed, but that you will be saved—and that by God." **(NIV)**

Big Idea: Don't be shocked when others oppose you for your faith.

---

1. Share an experience you have encountered while sharing your faith or someone you know? (Be specific) _____

_____

_____

_____

In our passage today, the Apostle Paul reminds the Philippians to not be shocked when others opposed them for being Christ followers. Implying something very important, that people will oppose us, at times, whether we like it or not. It is a matter fact that it will happen at one time or another. So, we shouldn't be alarmed when it does because it's not out of the norm. Look again at v. 28: *"Without being frightened in any way by those who oppose you."*

2. What kinds of opposition can a person expect when others realize we stand for Christian beliefs? (Explain your answers) _____

_____

_____

_____

Now, it might be helpful to think about this in the context of the language used. Notice what the Apostle Paul didn't say. He didn't say -if you are opposed don't be frightened. He didn't say -just in case you're opposed—don't be frightened. And he didn't mention: -maybe, you'll be opposed. It was given that it was going to happen at that church.

3. Describe what the following texts show about opposition to the faith?

Luke 11:53:	
Luke 23:2:	
Acts 18:6:	
1 Corinthians 16:9:	
2 Timothy 3:8:	
2 Timothy 4:15:	

The main text of our study today also implies that opposition will happen to us now for the same reasons.

Insight: We should persevere when we face opposition for our faith because believers before us did.

You may remember recently we noted that this was not a long-established church. Or one that was rooted for years and years. They were roughly six to 8 years old. As well as the first and only Christian church in that area, most likely. So, they understood perseverance firsthand in what they experienced building that church.

4. What do the following verses say about perseverance?

Romans 5:2-4:	
2 Thessalonians 1:4:	
Hebrews 12:1:	
James 1:2-4:	
James 5:11:	
2 Peter 1:6:	
Revelation 2:2:	
Revelation 2:19:	

Paul also mentions in v. 27b: "I will know that you are standing together with one spirit and one purpose, fighting together for the faith, which is the Good News." So, if believers before us in the history of the church faced difficulties, we should persevere also.

There are many ways that churches are opposed for their faith, both then in the church in Philippi and now. Don't be shocked if it happens to you, for your faith in Christ. Stand strong for Christ.

"If there is one doctrine, I have preached more than another, it is the doctrine of perseverance of the saints, even to the end." 2 Spurgeon

---

Let's stand strong for Christ when opposition arises from those around us.

Philippians-Joy in Action Study Guide

Challenge Section:

1. What opposition have I experienced as a Christian? _____
_____
_____

2. How did I respond?_____
_____
_____
_____

3. In what ways can I grow or improve my response and defend my
faith?_____
_____
_____
_____

Going Deeper Section:

Regarding verse 28, the NIV Study Bible expands by saying the following: "1:28 sign. Persistent opposition to the church and the gospel is a sure sign of eventual destruction, since it involves rejection of the only way of salvation. By the same token, when Christians are persecuted for their faith, this is a sign of the genuineness of their salvation (see 2Th 1:5 and note)." 3

Going Deeper Response:

Write down in detail the last opposition encounter you had while sharing your faith. Then think about and list possible: better, articulate, informed, and scriptural responses for the next time you experience opposition.

Close in Prayer...

_____

Lesson written by Pastor Frank & Samuel Gervasi

_____

1. Adapted from a story told on Illustration Ideas, https://illustrationideas.bible/unexpected-resistance//, as accessed on 1/19/2025.
2. Charles Spurgeon, https://www.princeofpreachers.org/quotes/category/perseverance-of-the-saints, as accessed on 01/19/2025
3. NIV Study Bible, Zondervan Copyright 2011, https://www.biblegateway.com/passage/?search=philippians%201%3A27-28&version=NIV, as accessed on)1/19/2025

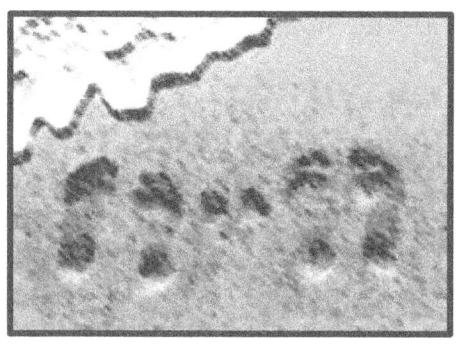

Lesson #8 - In the Footsteps of the Faithful
Read: *Philippians 1:28-29*

————————————

Memory Verse: *"Consider it pure joy, my brothers and sisters, whenever you face trials of many kinds, 3 because you know that the testing of your faith produces perseverance."* **James 1:2-3, NIV**

————————————

Open in Prayer:

Introduction:

"There is an interesting story about one evening when President Coolidge had company for dinner. He invited some friends from Vermont to join him for a meal at the White House. These visitors were worried about their table manners, so they decided to do everything their host did. All went well until coffee was served. Coolidge poured his into the saucer. The guests did the same. The President added sugar and cream. So did the visitors. Then Coolidge leaned over and placed his saucer on the floor for the cat." 1

Each of us walks in someone's footprints, following someone's example. But what if walking in the footsteps of the heroes of the faith means suffering, loss, and even death? As we'll see as we continue our emphasis on Philippians, sometimes suffering for the faith is inevitable.

Read Philippians 1:28-29

"Without being frightened in any way by those who oppose you. This is a sign to them that they will be destroyed, but that you will be saved—and that by God. 29 For it has been granted to you on behalf of Christ not only to believe in him, but also to suffer for him." **(NIV)**

Big Idea: When we suffer for knowing Christ, we are following the Biblical example of those before us, so we don't need to be discouraged.

In our passage today, the Apostle Paul continues his discussion about believers suffering for acknowledging Jesus as the Lord of their lives. He describes suffering in language that makes it sound almost like a gift from God.

1. What does it mean to suffer? (Explain your answers)

_____

_____

_____

Verse 29 says, *"For it has been granted to you on behalf of Christ not only to believe in him, but also to suffer for him." (NIV)*

2. What do the following verses show about suffering?

Matthew 16:21:	
Luke 9:22:	
Acts 5:41:	
Acts 9:16:	
Romans 8:17-18:	
Ephesians 3:13:	

Admittedly, these verses are not going to snag people easily into becoming a Christian. I don't think we'll ever hear this as a tag line for any evangelistic campaign. Nevertheless, it is a reality that goes with following Christ.

Insight: People have suffered for their faith over the years, so when you do, have courage that God has called you to walk through it also.

The apostles, the very men who walked and talked with Jesus during His earthly ministry, all met brutal and gruesome ends, apart from John.

Peter was crucified upside down in Rome. James, Jesus' younger brother, was thrown from the pinnacle of the Temple and beaten to death with a club. Bartholomew was flayed in Armenia. Thomas was run through with a spear in India.

3. What are some possible reasons Christians don't feel they should also suffer for their faith? (Be specific)

A. _____ B. _____

C. _____ C. _____

D. _____

Yet each of the Apostles that were listed, lived lives that left a lasting impact on the world, a legacy more valuable and distinguished than any secular businessman, politician, or military general. Each of these men were rescued from death several times before their time to die came. And each of these men were welcomed into heaven by Jesus Himself, likely greeting them with the words of Matthew 25:21: ""Well done, good and faithful servant! You have been faithful with a few things; I will put you in charge of many things. Come and share your master's happiness!"" (NIV)

4. List the prominent attitudes in the following verses?

Philippians 3:10:	
Colossians 1:24:	
1 Thessalonians 1:6:	
2 Thessalonians 1:5:	
2 Timothy 1:8:	
2 Timothy 1:12:	

5. What mindsets have I had towards suffering for the faith? (Explain your answers) ___

_____
_____
_____
_____

Challenge Section:

1. In what ways might I suffer for being a Christian?_____
_____
_____
_____
_____

2. How can I honor God with that situation?_____
_____
_____
_____
_____

3. List the mindsets that get in the way of suffering for the Gospel and make it harder:_____
_____
_____
_____
_____

Suffering for Christ is a reality of the faith, that all believers of all ages have experienced. Let's face it with boldness and courage and stand firm on the truth of Christ.

_____

"No matter what precautions we take, no matter how well we have put together a good life, no matter how hard we have worked to be healthy, wealthy, comfortable with friends and family, and successful with our career — something will inevitably ruin it."
3 Tim Keller

_____

Philippians-Joy in Action Study Guide

Going Deeper Section:

What does the word "suffering" mean biblically? The Encyclopedia of the Bible lists multiple connotations of the word used throughout Scripture, including the kind described by the Apostle Paul in our passage. They define this kind of suffering as testimonial suffering, and say the following regarding it:

"People who choose to live for righteousness in an evil world must expect suffering also from external sources. Service for the Savior runs counter to the aspirations of this world's powers. Followers of Christ may suffer 'for his sake' (Phil 1:29), 'for righteousness' sake' (1 Pet 3:14), 'for the kingdom of God' (2 Thess 1:5), 'for the gospel' (2 Tim 2:9), for resisting Satan (1 Pet 2:19), 'as a Christian' (4:16), and 'for the name' (Acts 5:41)... What response is appropriate when we experience suffering as a testimony to our unhypocritical trust in the Lord? Remembering Christ's example of endurance under stress, we shall follow in His steps (1 Pet 2:21). One should not forget the heroes of faith who 'suffered mocking and scourging, and even chains and imprisonment...' Like Moses, one may consider suffering abuse for Christ greater wealth than the treasures of Egypt (11:26). So believers shall complete the suffering necessary for the building of the Church (Col 1:24), knowing that it assures future glory (1 Pet 4:13)." 2

Going Deeper Response:

Find stories of people who have been martyred or suffered for sharing the Gospel on the mission Field. Then pray for each one that stands out to you and commit to praying regularly for their ministry for the next week.

Pray: Thanking God for giving me the privilege to suffer for His name, and asking Him to give me strength and guidance to bear it well...

———————————————

Lesson written by Pastor Frank & Samuel Gervasi

1. Adapted from a story accessed on https://www.sermonillustrations.com/a-z/e/example.htm, on 1/23/2025.
2. Encyclopedia of the Bible, as accessed on Bible Gateway Plus, on 1/23/2025.
3. Desiring God, https://www.desiringgod.org/articles/20-quotes-from-walking-with-god-through-pain-and-suffering, as accessed on 06/23/2025.

Philippians-Joy in Action Study Guide

Philippians-Joy in Action Study Guide

Lesson #9 - God's Reward
Read: *Philippians 1:27-30*

_____

Memory Verse: *"Look, I am coming soon! My reward is with me, and I will give to each person according to what they have done." **Revelation 22:12, NIV***

_____

Open in Prayer:

_____

Introduction:

The Our Daily Bread devotion tells about an event, *"On December 16, 1944, eighteen members of a reconnaissance platoon held off a battalion of crack German storm troopers in the Belgian hamlet of Lanzerath. Few history books note that their gallant stand gave Allied forces time to begin mounting the defense that eventually won the famous Battle of the Bulge. One of the platoon members was Will James, who after the war slipped into oblivion for nearly 4 decades. During that time he underwent numerous painful surgeries as a result of his war wounds. Not until 1981, through the efforts of U.S. House Speaker Thomas P. O'Neill and columnist Jack Anderson, was he awarded, posthumously, the Distinguished Service Cross for extraordinary heroism.* [1]

Most people like receiving rewards for a job well done, or hard work in something. And, when we are speaking about matters of faith, it's the same way. Because we want to be rewarded in some way by God, that we have not done suffered or persevered for nothing. However, God works in His own and time and the way that He feels is best.

Philippians-Joy in Action Study Guide

Read Philippians 1:27-30:

"Then, whether I come and see you or only hear about you in my absence, I will know that you stand firm in the one Spirit,[a] striving together as one for the faith of the gospel 28 without being frightened in any way by those who oppose you. This is a sign to them that they will be destroyed, but that you will be saved—and that by God. 29 For it has been granted to you on behalf of Christ not only to believe in him, but also to suffer for him, 30 since you are going through the same struggle you saw I had and now hear that I still have." (NIV)

_____

Big Idea: The Reward of our faithfulness to live the Christian life will come from God.

_____

1. What types of things come to your mind when you consider rewards? (explain your answers)_____
_____
_____
_____

In our passage today, the Apostle Paul continues his discussion about believers and suffering but also that believers will be blessed by God Himself. If you think about it anytime, we do anything for God, there will always be a reward of some kind or another. And in this case, it could be a couple of different possibilities regarding suffering for their faith. However, God was the one who was going to bless the Philippians. It says in v. 28b: "This is a sign to them that they will be destroyed, but that you will be saved—and that by God." (NIV). The word "salvation" as it is used here is not necessarily speaking about rescued from the kingdom of darkness but may be more in the saving in a general sense.

2. What were individuals saved from according to the following verses?

Exodus 14:30:	
Exodus 18:4:	
Judges 2:18:	
2 Samuel 22:4:	
Psalm 18:3:	
Psalm 106:8:	

The Interlinear Bible defines the word as: "deliverance, preservation, safety." 2 So, maybe speaking about being rescued from the hardships they were experiencing.

Nevertheless, it is also implying that God was the one bringing the reward, even if that meant the blessing was being rescued.

_____

Insight: The reward of God may not be like we think or immediately -however it will come in due season.

_____

3. What might be some reasons someone may think God is taking long to respond to prayers, requests, or rewarding faithfulness? (Be specific)

A. _____ B. _____
C. _____ D. _____

We all like receiving gifts and rewards for faithfulness in some areas. However, when it comes to God it may be in a future season. Nevertheless, it will always arrive and in unplanned ways.

4. What do the following Texts show about faithfulness?

Genesis 32:9-11:	
1 Samuel 26:23:	
2 Samuel 22:4:	
Psalm 36:5:	
Lamentations 3:22-24:	

We sometimes like to dictate how God will bless us, but His ways are beyond us and our ways of thinking.

5. What are some ways God has blessed you or answered prayer in the past? (Explain your answers) _____
_____
_____
_____
_____

The reward may also be just experiencing full salvation at a future time, when we will see Him face-to-face. Let us persevere in doing all things for Christ, regardless of what that may be.

What do the following verses show about salvation?

Acts 13:47:	
Romans 1:16:	
2 Corinthians 7:10:	
Ephesians 1:13:	
1 Thessalonians 5:9:	

———————————

"Our rewards in heaven are a result of God's crowning His own gifts." 3 Augustine

———————————

The reward will come at the right time, and in the correct way.

———————————

Challenge Section:

1. In what ways can I be faithful in the Christian life? _____
_____
_____
_____

2. What might God have in store for me? _____
_____
_____
_____

3. What rewards do I like seeing for people? _____
_____
_____
_____

Philippians-Joy in Action Study Guide

Going Deeper Section:

What does the idea of sharing our faith bring? The CSB Tony Evans Study Bible lists sharing our faith as the most important honor a believer can have. He says: "1:28 Courage is crucial to our gospel witness. God, the sovereign King, can embolden failing hearts and eradicate stumbling blocks. Don't be frightened by opponents of the good news....in.... 1:29 Suffering may appear to be a strange gift, but it's not. Suffering for the sake of Christ is purposeful, not purposeless. He allows it for our good and for his glory—and that makes all the difference." 4

Going Deeper Response:

Take a concordance and look up the word rewards or blessings. Identify what the reward was for the people or how they were blessed. Then thank God for His faithfulness.

Pray: Thanking God to bless us in the right season and how He sees fit....

———————————

Lesson written by Pastor Frank & Samuel Gervasi

———————————

1. Adapted from a story accessed at: https://www.sermonillustrations.com/a-z/r/rewards.htm, as accessed on)1/26/2025.
2. Interlinear Bible, https://www.biblestudytools.com/interlinear-bible/nas/philippians/passage/?q=philippians%201%3A27-30, as accessed on 1/26/2025.
3. Augustine, Quote Fancy, https://quotefancy.com/quote/905945/Saint-Augustine-Our-rewards-in-heaven-are-a-result-of-God-s-crowning-His-own-gifts, as accessed on 01/26/2025.
4. Tony Evans, CSB Study Bible, Holman, Copyright © 2017 by Holman Bible Publishers, www.biblegateway.com, as accessed on)1/26/2025.

Philippians-Joy in Action Study Guide

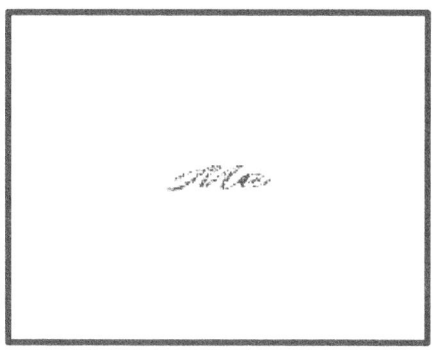

Lesson #10 - The Big M-E
Read: *Philippians 2:1-4*

Memory Verse: *"Because of the privilege and authority God has given me, I give each one of you this warning: Do not think you are better than you really are. Be honest in your evaluation of yourselves, measuring yourselves by the faith God has given us."* ***Romans 12:3, NIV***

Open in Prayer:

Introduction:

"Harry Ironside was a Canadian preacher and former pastor of Moody Church in Chicago, an accomplished man in ministry to say the least. But despite this, at times, Ironside would become convicted about his lack of humility. So, it was said that a friend recommended as a remedy, that he march through the streets of Chicago wearing a sandwich board, shouting the Scripture verses written on the board for all to hear. Dr. Ironside agreed to this venture and did that very thing – yelling them loudly one after another and making a spectacle of himself. Eventually, he finished his task and returned to his study. He removed the sandwich board, sat down, put his feet up, and thought, "I'll bet there's not another man in town who would have done that." 1

Dr. Ironside wasn't the only one who found it easy to think too highly of himself. Humility is something we all will struggle to maintain at times during our walk with Christ. As we continue in our emphasis on the book of Philippians, we will see in our passage today, how putting others first is intrinsically related to cultivating a humble heart.

<u>Read Philippians 2:1-4:</u>

"Therefore if you have any encouragement from being united with Christ, if any comfort from his love, if any common sharing in the Spirit, if any tenderness and compassion, 2 then make my joy complete by being like-minded, having the same love, being one in spirit and of one mind. 3 Do nothing out of selfish ambition or vain conceit. Rather, in humility value others above yourselves, 4 not looking to your own interests but each of you to the interests of the others." **(NIV)**

Big Idea: Humility means putting the needs and concerns of others higher than our own.

In our passage today, the Apostle Paul links a humble mindset to what we value more: others or ourselves. Verses 3-4 say, *"Do nothing out of selfish ambition or vain conceit. Rather, in humility value others above yourselves, not looking to your own interests but each of you to the interests of others."* (NIV)

1. What do you think putting others needs before your own means? (Explain your answer)

_____
_____
_____
_____

Thinking of others is important for probably several reasons but most importantly we should do it because the Scriptures admonish us to do so.

2. What do the following verses show about pride?

2 Chronicles 26:16:	
Psalm 10:4:	
Psalm 31:18	
Proverbs 16:18:	
Ezekiel 28:2:	
1 John 2:16:	

When it comes to combatting pride it's important to be purposeful as well as seeking to live by the Holy Spirit. Because pride is naturally self-centered and self-oriented.

Philippians-Joy in Action Study Guide

Pride is all about a two-letter word: M and E – but humility is others-oriented, thinking less of ourselves and more of the people around us.

3. What ways can pride manifest/show itself in the life of people usually? (Be specific)

_____
_____
_____
_____

_____

Insight: One of the main characteristics of someone who is walking in humility is looking out for the interests of others, so we should aim to emulate this quality in our own walk with God!

_____

Oftentimes, people confuse humility with weakness or a lack of self-esteem. But low self-esteem is not the same as biblical humility.

4. What do the following texts show about humility?

2 Samuel 22:28:	
2 Kings 22:19:	
2 Chronicles 7:14:	
2 Chronicles 12:7:	
Psalm 18:27:	
Psalm 25:9:	

"True humility is not to think low of oneself but to think rightly of oneself." Unknown

Notice the connotation behind the phrase "vain conceit". This phrase comes from a Greek word that means "vain glory, groundless, empty pride". 2

5. What are ways to help assure we don't let pride set in? (Be specific)

A. _____   B. _____
C. _____   D. _____
E. _____

May these words never describe us as ambassadors of Christ! Let's choose to turn away from the hollowness of pride and choose to be humble, let's think more others' needs than our own appearances, and let's allow the Spirit of God to teach us how to think rightly of ourselves.

Challenge Section:

1. What does it mean to think rightly of myself? _____
_____
_____
_____

2. How can I focus on others' needs first and foremost today? _____
_____
_____
_____

3. What ways have I allowed pride to set in? _____
_____
_____
_____

Going Deeper Section:

When we fail to value others' needs above our own, our prideful hearts will push too hard to have our own needs (or wants) met and end up destroying relationships and creating rivalry along the way. But humility is the antidote for rivalry. In the ESV Reformation Study Bible, we see this very truth being discussed:
"Pride is competitive by nature and tries to lift a person above others, so promoting conflicts rather than harmony (vv. 2, 14; 1:27). By contrast, humility accepts a place of service, with concern for the needs and interests of others (v. 4). Love (v. 2) is essential for humility (1:9; 1 Cor. 13:4, 5)." *3*

Going Deeper Response:

Identify an area or person where you were prideful with. Then lift the situation up in prayer. Then contact them to seek resolution or restoration in that relationship.

Close in Prayer: Asking God to cultivate in me a humble heart for His glory...

—————————————

Lesson written by Pastor Frank & Samuel Gervasi

—————————————

1. Adapted from a story accessed on https://sermoncentral.com/sermon-illustrations/20206/dr-harry-ironside-a-renowned-preacher-of-the-by-sermon-central, on 1/30/2024.
2. Interlinear Bible, https://www.biblestudytools.com/lexicons/greek/kjv/kenodoxia.html, as accessed on 1/30/2025.
4. ESV Reformation Study Bible, Copyright © 2015 by P & R Publishing, generously provided by Ligonier Ministries, www.biblegateway.com, as accessed on 1/30/2025.

Lesson #11 - Serving Models Christ
Read: *Philippians 2:5-8*

Memory Verse: *"Now that I, your Lord and Teacher, have washed your feet, you also should wash one another's feet. I have set you an example that you should do as I have done for you."* **John 13:14-15 NIV**

Open in Prayer:

Introduction:

A story was told about D.L Moody and exercising humility through service. It was said: "A large group of European pastors came to one of D. L. Moody's Northfield Bible Conferences in Massachusetts in the late 1800s. Following the European custom of the time, each guest put his shoes outside his room to be cleaned by the hall servants overnight. But of course, this was America and there were no hall servants. Walking the dormitory halls that night, Moody saw the shoes and determined not to embarrass his brothers. He mentioned the need to some ministerial students who were there but met with only silence or pious excuses. Moody returned to the dorm, gathered up the shoes, and, alone in his room, the world-famous evangelist began to clean and polish the shoes. Only the unexpected arrival of a friend amid the work revealed the secret. When the foreign visitors opened their doors the next morning, their shoes were shining. They never knew by whom. Moody told no one, but his friend told a few people, and during the rest of the conference, different men volunteered to shine the shoes in secret.1

Humility is shown through service to others around us. Just like in the story of D.L. Moody, we also show humility when we humble ourselves and serve others. As we continue in our emphasis in the book of Philippians, we see that Christ was the greatest servant of all, leaving an example for us today.

Philippians-Joy in Action Study Guide

Read Philippians 2:5-8:

"In your relationships with one another, have the same mindset as Christ Jesus: 6 Who, being in very nature[a] God, did not consider equality with God something to be used to his own advantage; 7 rather, he made himself nothing by taking the very nature[b] of a servant, being made in human likeness.
8 And being found in appearance as a man, he humbled himself by becoming obedient to death— even death on a cross!" **(NIV)**

_____

Big Idea: A Humble Person Will Model Christ by Serving Others...

_____

1. Describe an important person/people in your spiritual journey that has/have served as a role-model(s)? *(Be specific)* _____
_____
_____
_____
_____

In our passage today, the Apostle Paul links a humble mindset to modeling Christ's behavior. Modeling was probably the most significant way that Christ taught during his earthly ministry. Verse 5 says, "have the same mindset as Christ Jesus had." (NIV).

2. Why do you think modeling a behavior can be so powerful? *(Explain your answers)* _
_____
_____
_____
_____

During his three years of ministry, he did that very thing with his own disciples. In fact, they did everything together. They ate together, lived together, worshiped together, even travelled and ministered together also.

3. What stands out in the following texts about modeling something?

1 Samuel 6:5:	
1 Samuel 6:11:	
Luke 11:1-3:	
Philippians 3:17:	
1 Thessalonians 1:7:	
2 Thessalonians 3:9:	

Philippians-Joy in Action Study Guide

So, by implication they also served each other as well. Because also in verse 5, the apostle Paul noted: *"In your relationships with each with one another."* So, it was in essence telling them to serve those around them, and they were around each other the most. In addition to the various people, they encountered.

Insight: *One of the main characteristics of someone who is walking in humility is serving others. Jesus did and so should we....*

---

4. What could be some ways we can serve others in the faith? *(Be specific)*

A. _____ B. _____
C. _____ D. _____
E. _____

It was noted that: oftentimes, people confuse humility with weakness. And humility is not only thinking right of oneself but also shown through service to others. However, because Christ modelled it servanthood to his disciples, we should also serve those around us today.

5. What do the following texts show about humility? *(Be specific)*

Proverbs 11:2:	
Proverbs 22:4:	
Zephaniah 2:3:	
Acts 20:19:	
James 3:13:	
1 Peter 5:5:	

The highlighted verse from John chapter 13 shows humility in service as well. In fact, if Jesus the Son of God was not too prideful to serve his own disciples, it should serve as our best example to do the same. In John 13:14-15 it shows: "Now that I, your Lord and Teacher, have washed your feet, you also should wash one another's feet. I have set you an example that you should do as I have done for you." Think about how he got up from the table, putting on an outer garment and stooping down to do something as simple as washing a person's feet, and how it speaks at such volume.

In fact, Peter is beside himself and wants no part of it. In John 13 he says: "He came to Simon Peter, who said to him, 'Lord, are you going to wash my feet?'.....'No,' said Peter, 'you shall never wash my feet.'" (NIV, vv. 6, 8).

6. What could be some reasons people can view serving others as Peter might have?
(Explain your answers) _____
_____
_____
_____
_____

Humility will always be shown through service to others. My we follow our Lord's example and serve those around us.

Challenge Section:

1. Have I walked in humility lately? _____
_____
_____
_____

2. Who can I serve to model Christ's humility today?
_____
_____
_____
_____

3. How can I serve those people I listed? _____
_____
_____
_____

Philippians-Joy in Action Study Guide

When we model Christ's behavior it becomes clear to see he was a true servant in every sense of the word. Even though he was the Son of God and God in human form, serving was not beneath him. In the Zondervan Illustrated Bible Backgrounds Commentary of the New Testament, we see this very truth being shown: "Taking the very nature of a servant (2:7). The word translated "servant" in the niv is the common word for "slave" (see comments on 1:1). But in what sense did Jesus take the form of a slave? From the standpoint of the Romans, Jesus was a common Jew, a member of a people whom the Roman general Pompey had conquered in 63 b.c. and over whom the Romans had ruled ever since, sometimes directly through governors and sometimes indirectly through puppet kings such as Herod the Great, his son Archelaeus, and his grandson Herod Agrippa I. From the Jewish perspective, however, rule by a foreign power was slavery—well-deserved punishment for breaking God's law (Deut. 28:68; Ezra 9:9). Jesus became just such a slave, sharing the curse of the law that had fallen on God's people (Gal. 3:10; 4:4), although he alone among God's people had broken none of God's laws." 2

Going Deeper Response:

Contact your closest shelter, Food Pantry, or Retirement Community and decisively reach out and schedule a time to serve there....

Pray: Asking God to cultivate in me a humble heart for His glory by serving others...

_____

Lesson written by Pastor Frank & Samuel Gervasi

_____

1. Adapted from a story accessed on https://bible.org/illustration/man-servant%E2%80%99s-heart, on 02/02/2024.
2. Zondervan Illustrated Bible Backgrounds Commentary of the New Testament, Copyright 2002, BibleGateway Plus, https://www.biblegateway.com/passage/?search=Philippians%202%3A5-8&version=NIV, as accessed on 02/02/2025.

Lesson #12 - Humility Is a Choice
Read: *Philippians 2:5-8*

Memory Verse: *"And being found in appearance as a man, he humbled himself by becoming obedient to death – even death on a cross!"* ***Philippians 2:8 NIV***

Open in Prayer:

> "There was a U.S. soldier by the name of William Edward Adams who was posthumously awarded the Medal of Honor. Stationed in the province of Kontum during the Vietnam War, Major Adams distinguished himself on May 25, 1971, while serving as a helicopter pilot. On that date...Adams volunteered to fly a lightly armed helicopter... to a small fire base under attack by a large enemy force...to evacuate three seriously wounded soldiers. There were numerous antiaircraft weapons around the base that the enemy had overrun, but Adams volunteered to rescue his comrades anyway. As he approached the base, the enemy gunners opened fire with heavy machine guns. Undaunted by the fusillade, he continued his approach, landed the aircraft at the fire base, and patiently waited until the wounded soldiers were placed on board. As Adams' helicopter took off to return to home base, it was struck and seriously damaged by the enemy. Adams attempted a safe crash landing, but despite his valiant efforts, the helicopter exploded, and Adams and the wounded soldiers he came to save lost their lives." [1]

> William Adams knew before he got into his helicopter that the odds were stacked against him, and the chances of returning successfully weren't in his favor. But he chose to fly in anyway. He made a conscious decision to humbly lay his own life on the line for the well-being of others. There is Another who also laid His life on the line, not to save us from bombs and bullets, but from the penalty of our sin. And as we'll see in our passage today, Jesus' decision to go the cross serves as an example to us, that we too must decide to be humble.

Read: *Philippians 2:5-8*

"In your relationships with one another, have the same mindset as Christ Jesus: 6 Who, being in very nature[a] God, did not consider equality with God something to be used to his own advantage; 7 rather, he made himself nothing by taking the very nature[b] of a servant, being made in human likeness. 8 And being found in appearance as a man, he humbled himself by becoming obedient to death— even death on a cross!" **(NIV)**

―――――――――――

Big Idea: In the same way Christ chose to give His life for us, we must make a conscious choice to humbly put others first.

―――――――――――

1. Do you think that building biblical traits comes automatically or we must pursue? (Explain you answers) _____
_____
_____
_____

2. What areas might require more diligence than others on regards to spiritual growth?

A. _____ B. _____
C. _____ D. _____
E. _____

In our passage today, the Apostle Paul gives us an example of what true humility looks like. Notice how he says in verses 7-8: *"Rather, he made himself nothing by taking the very nature of a servant, being made in human likeness. And being found in appearance as a man, he humbled himself by becoming obedient to death – even death on a cross!"* (NIV)

Notice how Paul uses the word "humbled" as a verb – implying action! We must choose to show humility.

3. What do the following texts say about a person's actions?

Proverbs 20:11:	
Jeremiah 4:18:	
Jeremiah 7:3-5:	
Ezekiel 20:43:	
Acts 7:22:	
Galatians 6:4:	

This idea of an action verb is reiterated in verse 7 when he says Christ "made himself" nothing, again implying a conscious resolve to do so by His own free will. Humility is not something that comes naturally to us; we must actively cultivate a humble heart!

4. What role does the holy Spirit play in spiritual growth? (Explain) _____

_____
_____
_____
_____

Even though the holy Spirit is key in our growth, the easier areas for us individually, should be tackled and can come by taking action also. It's sometimes when we step forward in faith and try by taking action, that God meets us and helps us in powerful ways.

_____

Insight: Because Christ gave up the glories of heaven to save our souls, we should lay down our pride and serve others humbly in love.

_____

Notice the exclamation at the end of verse 8: "…even death on a cross!" (NIV) Death by crucifixion was usually reserved for criminals, so it was a shameful, and humbling, way to die. But Christ made that choice to give up His divine privileges to redeem us!

5. Look up the following texts and list whether the action was God or man taking action with their pride:

2 Chronicles 32:26:	
Proverbs 14:3:	
Ezekiel 28:2:	
Daniel 4:37:	
1 John 2:16:	

Philippians-Joy in Action Study Guide

And in spite of all of Major William Adams' bravery in Vietnam, because of his human limitations, he was unable to save those he came for. But through the limitless power of God, Christ successfully purchased us through the cross and rescued those He came to die for. And we are called, as His children, to display the same selfless humility toward others.

F.B. Meyers, a friend of D.L. Moody and evangelist in England, once said this: "I used to think that God's gifts were on shelves one above another, and the taller we grow, the easier we can reach them........ 2

".......Now I find that God's gifts are on shelves one beneath another, and the lower we stoop, the more we get." 2 F.B. Meyers

---

Challenge Section:

1. How can I keep myself from becoming prideful today? _____
_____
_____
_____

2. In what new ways can I humbly serve those around me? _____
_____
_____
_____

3. What areas are hardest for me to serve others in?

A. _____ *B.* _____
C. _____ *D.* _____
D. _____ *E.* _____

Philippians-Joy in Action Study Guide

Going Deeper Section:

Just how much humility did it take for Jesus to die for our sins? In the ESV Global Study Bible, we see the extent of Christ's humility in the following excerpt:

"It is remarkable enough that God the Son would take on human form for a broken world. But Jesus went much farther, becoming obedient (compare Rom. 5:19) to the point of death, even death on a cross. Crucifixion was the ultimate humiliation, and the physical pain was terrible (see note on Matt. 27:35). It was the total opposite of the divine majesty of the preexistent Christ. Thus, it was the ultimate expression of Christ's obedience to the Father." 3

Going Deeper Response

Take your bible and identify 3 people that served others. Then after looking them up, pray asking God to open doors for similar service opportunities this week.......

Pray: Thanking God for saving me, and asking Him to help me grow in humble service...

_____

Lesson written by Pastor Frank & Samuel Gervasi

_____

1. Adapted from a story accessed on https://www.cmohs.org/recipients/william-e-adams, on 2/06/2024.
2. Quote by F.B. Meyer, adapted by Andrew Murray in Humility: The Journey Towards Holiness. https://www.goodreads.com/quotes/7272326-i-used-to-think-that-god-s-gifts-were-on-shelves-one.
3. ESV Global Study Bible, Copyright © 2012 by Crossway. All rights reserved. As accessed at BibleGateway Plus, https://www.biblegateway.com/passage/?search=philippians%202%3A5-8&version=NIV, on 02/06/2025.

Lesson #13 - Humility Is Rewarded
Read: *Philippians 2:9-11*

Memory Verse: *"But he gives us more grace. That is why Scripture says: 'God opposes the proud but shows favor to the humble.'"* ***James 4:6 NIV***

Open in Prayer:

Introduction:

I once heard a story about Edward Stanton who, "was a lawyer and politician who served as Abraham Lincoln's secretary of war during the American Civil War. Stanton was a close ally of Lincoln and played a key role in the Union's war effort." 1 However, rumors had circulated that during the war Lincoln made a choice by issuing a command that affected Stanton. Consequently, Lincoln's trusted friend didn't immediately follow the order. In fact, Stanton was said to call him a fool! However, when Lincoln heard of what he was called, his reply was "then I must be acting like one." And, after the two talked, he heard the logic, and in humility, and rescinded the order. 2.

Read: Philippians 2:9-11

"Therefore God exalted him to the highest place and gave him the name that is above every name, 10 that at the name of Jesus every knee should bow, in heaven and on earth and under the earth, 11 and every tongue acknowledge that Jesus Christ is Lord, to the glory of God the Father." ***(NIV)***

Big Idea: A Humble Person is rewarded by God Himself.

1. What do you think it means to exalt something? (Explain) _____
_____
_____
_____

In our passage today, the Apostle Paul gives us an important reason for a person to show humility like Christ, that God Himself rewards it. Now, if we think about that, we see that God, himself will work on behalf of the person who is making the conscious choice of lowering themselves by walking and operating in a humble spirit. In fact, we get to experience the joy and peace that comes with that choice.

2. What are things people elevate today instead of God?

A. _____ B. _____
C. _____ D. _____
E. _____

Notice what he says in verse 9, "Therefore, God elevated Him to the place of highest honor." The elevating was done by someone greater. In this case God did because of the act of submission. Which by implication, is that God will do the same for those who choose this trait in their own lives.

3. Look up the following texts and identify who or what was being exalted?

Exodus 15:1-2:	
Numbers 2:47:	
1 Samuel 2:7:	
Chronicles 14:2:	
1 Chronicles 17:17:	

Now, for clarification, obviously exalts people to a different place of honor because this was speaking of the Second Person of the Trinity. Doing what was required to reconcile man back to God and restore all that was destroyed by the Fall of Man. However, I believe, God desires to reward those who walk in humility as well.

4. What are ways God can exalt a person to a place of honor? *(Explain your answer)* __

_____
_____
_____
_____

_____

Insight: We Should Strive for Humility Not Only Because It's Rewarded, but Also, to Avoid God's Opposition.

_____

Meaning, that God Himself will actively work against the person who is walking in pride. In fact, if we look again at our highlighted verse in James chapter 4, we can see it. Because it says: "But he gives us more grace. That is why Scripture says: 'God opposes the proud but shows favor to the humble.'"

5 What types of ways can God allow us to experience opposition?

A. _____ B. _____
C. _____ D. _____
E. _____

6. In what way do the following texts show the manner of opposition they experienced?

Numbers 16:42:	
Judges 9:25:	
Nehemiah 4:1:	
Acts 6:9:	
Thessalonians 2:2:	

The opposite of God allowing opposition is His grace. *Who wouldn't want to experience the grace of God in greater measure?* It would be a battle that everyone would lose if God were opposing them.

May we choose humility and experience the blessings of God's grace in our lives today!

_____

Challenge Section:

1. How can I keep myself from becoming prideful today? _____
_____
_____

2. What practical ways can I walk in humility? _____
_____
_____

3 What areas are hardest for me to remain humble? _____
_____
_____
_____

Going Deeper Section:

What was Christ exulted to? In the **Zondervan Illustrated Bible**, we see the response of God the Father because of the humility exhibited by Christ.

"Exaltation of Christ. The term covers the sequence of events that begins with the Resurrection of Christ and that includes his Ascension and his coming again (see Eschatology). The outcome of his humility and obedience, the "high exaltation" of Christ, will in turn lead to the bowing of every knee and the acknowledgment of his Lordship by every tongue (Phil. 2:8-11; cf. Acts 2:33). The exaltation of Christ places him "at the right hand of God" (Rom. 8:34), an expression used by Stephen (Acts 7:55-56), Paul (Eph. 1:20), Peter (1 Pet. 3:22), and the writer to the Hebrews (Heb. 1:3; 10:12; 12:2). This firmly establishes the association of Christ with God in power and glory, a glorification noted by our Lord himself (Jn. 17:5; cf. 12:32)." 3

Going Deeper Response:

Do an evaluation of the areas you give a higher priority in your life than you feel you should. Then after identified, bring them in prayer to God asking for the strength and wisdom to change....

Pray: *Asking God for more of His grace in our lives by choosing to avoid prideful living.*

———————————

Lesson written by Pastor Frank & Samuel Gervasi

———————————

1.Wikipedia,https://www.google.com/search?q=abraham+lincoln+and+edward+stanton&oq=abraham+lincoln+and+edward+stanton&gs_lcrp=EgZjaHJvbWUyBggAEEUYOTINCAEQABiGAxiABBiKBTINCAIQABiGAxiABBiKBTINCAMQABiGAxiABBiKBTIKCAQQABiABBiiBDIKCAUQABiABBiiBDIKCAYQABiiBBiJBdIBCTE2NTUwajBqNKgCALACAQ&sourceid=chrome&ie=UTF-8, on 2/06/2024.
2. Adapted by a story on, https://sermoncentral.com/sermon-illustrations/67817/abraham-lincoln-s-secretary-of-war-edwin-by-ajai-prakash, as accessed on 02/08/2025.
3. Bible Gateway Plus, https://www.biblegateway.com/passage/?search=Philippians%202%3A9-11&version=NIV, as accessed on 02/08/2025.

Philippians-Joy in Action Study Guide

88 | P a g e

Philippians-Joy in Action Study Guide

Lesson #14 - Obedience is Hard Work
Read: *Philippians 2:12-13*

_____

Memory Verse: "Do your best to present yourself to God as one approved, a worker who does not need to be ashamed and who correctly handles the word of truth." *2 Timothy 2:15, NIV*

_____

Open in Prayer:

Introduction:

"In May 2013, thirteen-year-old Arvind Mahankali correctly spelled the word kneidel (a German-Yiddish word for a dumpling) to win the 86th Scripps National Spelling Bee. Mahankali had finished third each of the two previous years, during which he was eliminated for failing to correctly spell a German-derived word. So, in preparation for his third attempt at the prize, Mahankali diligently worked to strengthen his area of weakness. 'This year I prepared German words, and I studied them, so when I got German words this year, I wasn't worried,' he said after his victory. No one has yet invented a way of acquiring...anything worthwhile—without effort." 1

Sometimes, in our walk with Christ, there will come times when we need to work hard to strive for spiritual growth. We were called to train ourselves to live godly lives, even when it doesn't come easily. And as we'll see in our passage today, this kind of hard work is crucial if we are to live a life that glorifies God appropriately.

Read: *Philippians 2:12-13*

Philippians-Joy in Action Study Guide

"Therefore, my dear friends, as you have always obeyed—not only in my presence, but now much more in my absence—continue to work out your salvation with fear and trembling, 13 for it is God who works in you to will and to act in order to fulfill his good purpose." (NIV)

———————————

Big Idea: We should press hard into matters of the faith, to do our best and live a life that honors God.

———————————

1. What do you think it means to honor something or someone? *(Explain your answer(s)* _____

_____

_____

_____

In our passage today, the Apostle Paul challenges the believers to continue being obedient, even though he is not present with those believers. He says it's important, in verse 12, that they, "Work hard to show the results of your salvation, obeying God with deep reverence and fear." (NLT)

2. What are some common reasons people honor someone?

A. _____ B. _____

C. _____ D. _____

E. _____

Every season of a believer's life should be one of deliberately working and applying the truths of Scripture to our own experiences, to live out our faith.

3. What do the following texts give as the underlying reasons for honoring others?

Genesis 30:20:	
Exodus 20:12:	
Judges 9:16:	
1 Samuel 2:29:	
1 Samuel 15:12:	
2 Samuel 1:2:	

Philippians-Joy in Action Study Guide

4. Do you think there are good reasons to honor another person? (Explain your answer (s) _____

_____

_____

_____

_____

Insight: Christ-followers should press hard into the Christian faith to worship God through their obedient actions.

_____

Verse 12 says to work hard "with deep reverence and fear" (NLT). Some versions translate this phrase, "with fear and trembling" (NIV). This second phrasing has led some to interpret these verses to say new believers should not be overly confident in their faith. But the phrase "with deep reverence and fear" sheds a different light on this verse. We work hard not out of fear or uncertainty whether our faith is genuine, but from a place of awe and amazement at the mercy God has shown to us.

5. What ways can we show awe and reverence towards God?

A. _____ B. _____
C. _____ D. _____
E. _____

Finally, it's important to note that Paul's exhortation to work hard in our faith is not suggesting we try to do right by our own power, or by following rules. That would contradict the Gospel, and our passage itself says, *"For God is working in you, giving you the desire and the power to do what pleases him."*

6. Identify who is working in the following texts:

John 5:17:	
1 Corinthians 12:6:	
Ephesians 3:7:	
Colossians 2:12:	
Colossians 3:23:	
Colossians 4:13:	

Philippians-Joy in Action Study Guide

But just because God is working in us to become more like Him, does not change the fact that we must train ourselves spiritually. In fact, it demonstrates faith that God will help us grow when we discipline ourselves to do right.

We must press hard into the things of God, going all in on living like Jesus. And with the power of the Holy Spirit working in us, we can live a life that Jesus wants.

Challenge Section:

1. What are the motivations behind why I do the right thing?_____
_____
_____
_____

2. In what area can I discipline myself to be godly today?_____
_____
_____
_____
_____

3. What has motivated me up until now in life?_____
_____
_____
_____

Going Deeper:

What does it mean that God works in us? In the 2nd edition of his *NKJV Study Bible*, John MacArthur elaborates on this phrase:

"Although the believer is responsible to work (v. 12), the Lord actually produces the good works and spiritual fruit in the lives of believers (John 15:5; 1 Cor. 12:6). This is accomplished because He works through us by His indwelling Spirit (Acts 1:8; 1 Cor. 3:16, 17; 6:19, 20; cf. Gal. 3:3)…God energizes both the believer's desires and his actions. The Gr. word for 'will' indicates that He is not focusing on mere desires or whimsical emotions, but on the studied intent to fulfill a planned purpose. God's power makes His church willing to live godly lives (cf. Ps. 110:3)."[2]

Pray: Asking God to give me the desire and the strength to do what pleases Him...

Lesson written by Pastor Frank & Samuel Gervasi

---

1. Adapted from a story accessed at https://ministry127.com/resources/illustration/the-necessity-of-preparation, on 2/13/2024.

2. NKJV MacArthur Study Bible, 2nd Edition, Copyright © 1997, 2006, 2019 by Thomas Nelson. All rights reserved. As accessed at Bible Gateway Plus, https://www.biblegateway.com/passage/?search=philippians%202%3A12-13&version=NIV, on 02/13/2025.

Philippians-Joy in Action Study Guide

Lesson #15 - Living Right is Crucial
Read: *Philippians 2:14-15*

Memory Verse: *"Live clean and innocent lives as children of God."* ***Philippians 2:15 NIV***

Open in Prayer:

Introduction:

"I read about an instant cake mix that was a big flop. The instructions said all you had to do was add water and bake. The company couldn't understand why it didn't sell -- until their research discovered that the buying public felt uneasy about a mix that required only water. Apparently, people thought it was too easy. So the company altered the formula and changed the directions to call for adding an egg to the mix in addition to the water. The idea worked and sales jumped dramatically." 1

It reminds me of our walk with Christ; we are called to live in ways that honor God. Unfortunately, we mix other things in with God's commands but all he is requiring that is that we live in ways without grumbling and complaining. Especially since people are constantly watching us because we claim to be Christ-followers.

Read: *Philippians 2:14-15*

"14 Do everything without grumbling or arguing, 15 so that you may become blameless and pure, "children of God without fault in a warped and crooked generation."[a] Then you will shine among them like stars in the sky." **(NIV)**

_____

Big Idea: Continuing in Joy Will Speak Volumes to Those Around Us.

_____

As we continue in our emphasis in Philippians, we see that when we continue in Joy, that it speaks volumes to others. So, if we like it or not, people are watching us both believers but also non-believers. So, because of that we should strive to be living in ways that brings God honor.

1. What ways can we bring honor to God? Especially, to those that see us and are not believers themselves? *(Be specific)* _____
_____
_____
_____

In our passage today, we can see in verse 14 that it says: *"Do everything without grumbling and complaining."* Now, that's a convicting thing to do if you think about it, depending on the situation. Many things can happen in life that rob our joy. Consequently, it's important that a believer is conscious and doesn't become discontented or complain.

2. What types of things do you tend to grumble and complain about?

A. _____ B. _____
C. _____ D. _____
E. _____

For other believers being conscious is important because it models how God wants us to behave in the World. Additionally, we should live without grumbling because non-believers will see it.

3. What types of things have you heard from non-believers regarding how Christians live? *(Explain your answer (s)* _____
_____
_____
_____

Philippians-Joy in Action Study Guide

4. List what you notice that the following texts say about grumbling:

Exodus 16:8-9:	
Numbers 14:27:	
Numbers 17:5:	
John 6:43:	
1 Peter 4:9:	

Insight: Christ-followers should live in a joyous way, so others don't criticize us and cast a bad light on Christianity.

5. What do you think it means for a Christian to live joyously? (Be specific) _____

_____

_____

_____

_____

Unfortunately, people will sometimes try and find fault with how a Christian lives and will use that as the excuse to not embrace the things of God. In verse 15 it says: *"So that no one can criticize you."* We should not give people a reason to accuse us of wrongdoing.

6. Read Acts 11:1-10 and describe what might have been the reason Peter was able to not get upset about those that were criticizing him? (Explain why) _____

_____

_____

_____

_____

Looking back in Philippians the Apostle Paul even goes further and gives us additional ways to live right. Because in the second part of verse 15 he says: *"Live clean and innocent lives as children of God."* Clean as used here is the idea of blameless but not perfect. Crooked as some versions use carries the idea of wicked. And, perverse is similar but really means wicked.

A.W. Tozer said it like this concerning right living: *"One of the most stinging criticisms made against Christians is that their minds are narrow and their hearts are small....that such a charge can be made at all is sufficient cause for serious heart searching and prayer."* 2

May we be people who live right before God, in joy, because others are watching our lives!

Challenge Section:

1. What does my life look like to those around me? _____

_____

_____

_____

2. In what ways do I need to grow and become more Christlike? _____

_____

_____

_____

3. What ways have I done well and living with a good testimony? _____

_____

_____

_____

Going Deeper Section:

What does it mean to live in the right ways? Sometimes it's easy to confuse the word blameless with perfection. However, it's not necessarily the same thing. In *the NIV Study Bible*, it elaborates on this question and idea:

"Blameless and pure . . . without fault. Not absolute, sinless perfection, but wholehearted, unmixed devotion to doing God's will (see 1:10 and note). warped and crooked generation. A description of the unbelieving world (see Ac 2:40; Eph 2:1–3; cf. Mt 17:17). shine among them like stars. The contrast, like light in darkness, that Christians are to be to the world around them (cf. Mt 5:15–16)." 3

Philippians-Joy in Action Study Guide

Pray: Asking God to give us the strength to live in upright ways and be more conscious of those around us......

———————————

Lesson written by Pastor Frank & Samuel Gervasi

———————————

1. Sermon Illustrations, https://www.sermonillustrations.com/a-z/w/works_righteousness.htm, as accessed on 2/16/2025.
2. Sermon titled: Shining Like Bright Lights for Christ, PFG, Original source unknown.
3. NIV Study Bible, Copyright © 1985, 1995, 2002, 2008, 2011 by Zondervan, accessed in Bible Study Tools on 02/16/2025.